7- Day Wage Garnishment Killer

The Death of a Wage Judgment

By: Yolonna Foxxe

7-Day Wage Garnishment Killer

The Death of a Wage Judgment

Copyright © 2018 by Yolonna Foxxe

All rights reserved. No part of this publication may be reproduced, distributed, or transmitted in any form or by any means, including photocopying, recording, or other electronic or mechanical methods, without the prior written permission of the publisher, except in the case of brief quotations embodied in critical reviews and certain other noncommercial uses permitted by copyright law. For permission requests, write to the publisher, addressed "Attention: Permissions Coordinator," at the address below.

ISBN-13:
978-1726075213

The Women's Book Shelf
16500 Joy Road-unit 66056
Detroit, MI 48228 Unit

Ordering Information:
Quantity sales. Special discounts are available on quantity purchases by corporations, associations, and others. For details, contact the publisher at the address above.
Orders by U.S. trade bookstores and wholesalers. Please contact The Women's Book Shelf LLC Tel: (248) 266-8076 or visit www.thewomensbookshelf.com

Printed in the United States of America

Cover Design by:
The Women's Bookshelf LLC
Informational E-books & Illustrations

Introduction:

The 7 Day Wage Garnishment Killer is a knockout book that will put a stop to bill collectors digging their sneaky little hands into your paycheck! There should be a law that prevents companies from having the right to cypher your hard earnings! But since these outrageous methods of pulling payments from your sole source of income is not outlawed you kind of have your hands tied. So, what do you do?

How can you stop wage garnishment in three days or more? A well-known method that people from all walks of life have used for years and I am sure is not new to you…is Bankruptcy! That's right if you have other debt that you can possibly include with this garnishment or maybe the garnishment itself is enormous enough to stand on its own in a bankruptcy case…then you may consider filing bankruptcy.

Filing for bankruptcy is not a trend like most people may believe. A lot of people are really in need of filing a bankruptcy to help to repair their lives. They may have credit issues, or they are trying to save their homes, could be they want to stop a garnishment or maybe they just simply want to start over.

However, the case may be bankruptcy is a very important legal step and should be deeply considered before making such a major move. So many people struggle with reoccurring bills, collections and other issues that may take a toll on their finances. Finding a way out of debt is hard especially if you must face the dilemma alone. What do you do? Many options come to mind but if you have immediate needs turning to bankruptcy wouldn't be such a bad choice.

I have heard so many horror stories about filing for bankruptcy.

Myth #1: If you file for bankruptcy you won't be able to apply for credit again…not true. You will find that so many finance companies will attempt to beat down your door begging for you to ruin your credit again…don't do it.

Myth #2: If you file bankruptcy on your own and you misspell your name you will face consequences…not true. Don't let tales like this scare you from filing your own bankruptcy; we all make mistakes and the courts understand and always allow you to correct your mistakes before and after you submit your application.

The list of myths and answers could go on and on, but the negative issues are not why we are here today and the reason that you picked this book as a guide to assist you in removing garnishments in three days or less. If you are faced with a wage garnishment and it drains your paycheck on a weekly or a bi-weekly basis then this is the book for you. If you feel like you are working to pay off your debt and sometimes you just want to quit, you job and just say forget it…this is the book that will help you get back to your life.

What can this book do for you? We will walk you through step by step on how to utilize the laws of bankruptcy to help to stop your wage garnishment almost instantly! Is this a gimmick? No…and you don't have to trust me because you don't really know me, but if you research the facts that I have already placed in this book you will see the possibility of removing your garnishment. Now you can take your sweet time researching and stretch out the time it takes to stop the garnishment fast or you can just go through this handy and thorough book that shows you the how and the why.

Disclaimer: I am not a lawyer I do not give legal advice. This book is a mere reflection of what I did to remove garnishment from my life and how you can do the same. If any of these passages are in any way similar to legal advice it is unintentional and has been abstracted from legal websites which will be acknowledged in the back of the book.

I hope that this helps the masses and if you are interested in any other aspect of pro se bankruptcy feel free to check out some of my other publications.

- *Filing your own Bankruptcy* **(Available Now!)**
- *10 Reasons not to file bankruptcy* **(Coming Soon! Pre-order)**
- *Life after Pro Se Bankruptcy* **(Coming Soon! Pre-order)**
- *How to earn $250,000 per year processing bankruptcies* **(Coming Soon! Pre-order)**
- *15 Step-by-step Recipes to Mega-Wealth* **(Coming Soon! Pre-order)**

Seven Days or Less Garnishment Killer

Order or Pre-order your copy of these amazing and well written publications. You will have access to information that took me close to fifteen (15) years to put together! Although the Internet has a lot of free information, you must know the right questions to ask and I have the answers to questions you may not even knew to ask!

*Get your copy of my tell all books so that you can begin your journey to financial success whether its through starting over or earning a rewarding career; it's all here and more! If you order any of these books by the end of the year **2018** you will receive a free copy of **50 Fun Facts You May Not Know About Filing your Own Bankruptcy** and a **12-month E-mail subscription** that connects you to my blog **The Life Style of Thousandaire!***

So, without any more delay let's get started learning how to stop wage garnishment within 7 days or less! Read thoroughly; you will be glad that you did!

Seven Days or Less Garnishment Killer

Table of Contents:

What is a wage garnishment?..........................#07

Who can garnish your wages?........................ #16

How to stop a creditor from garnishing you…#25

How to File a Claim of Exemption?................#33

How to Prevent Wage Garnishment…............#40

7- Day Breakdown on killing a garnishment...#44

Conclusion….. #59

Glossary…... #63

What is a Wage Garnishment?

Okay so by now anybody who is anybody should know what a wage garnishment is. Especially if you are already experiencing one, there is no doubt that you know what is happening to your paycheck. But for those of you that may kind of know…but don't exactly know what it is and why it is allowed, I will explain as best I can in this chapter.

It's safe to say that as a human we all have made a lot of mistakes. Forgetting or neglecting to pay a bill, big or small is not uncommon for most of us. But there are times that we fall so far behind that we cannot catch up; creditors tacking on fees and interest makes it hard for a person to regain there financial footing. After awhile as life goes on we may put that bill on the back burner and make it a lost obligation. All the while the creditor has their job to do as they fill your payment history up with non-pays and delinquencies until finally they realize that you may not have any intention on paying them back. And then boom you're hit with a fat bill that you somehow forgot existed!

Let's just say that you may have waned to pay your bill, but it just became too much for you to bare. It's okay, it's no secret that we prioritize every day to live a lifestyle that we financially maintain by paying utility bills, insurances, car notes, mortgages; all the things that we need, things that matter most…well, we put those things first. To contemplate on a past due bill for something that we are not even using anymore is usually way at the bottom of our list. Right?

Then from out of nowhere without warning, (and this has happened on many occasions) your paycheck has an extra deduction that shrinks your hard-earned pay in half! You look closely at your check stub and begin to remember the debt that dreaded past due debt. That old bill suddenly becomes new again and creates a new a priority. Your "regular bills" vacation plans and big-ticket items are now taking a back seat to this once forgotten debt. It's the number one bill on your list because it's sponging off your pay and you must do something to get it under control!

Once you face the fact that you have lost wages, you begin to worry and wonder what to do about it. Do you just let them take it until they pay themselves off? Or do you fight and try to get to the bottom of the issue? The first thing you should do is stay calm and focus and research your rights in your state. Find out who is garnishing you and why if you really don't know. Know exactly what a wage judgment or wage garnishment is before you move forward.

From what I have researched a wage garnishment involves a lawsuit that is brought against you for money that you owe a creditor or debtor. Documents are filed with the court to begin proceedings to bring a money judgment against you and if the debtor wins or receives a default judgment. (if you fail to respond to the lawsuit) Basically a debtor cannot just collect money from your paycheck without getting consent from a judge after taking you to court. If you don't show up to court or respond to the summons by the due date you will lose by default and your job will be ordered to pay your creditor with your wages.

Wage judgments can hit unexpectedly if you owe a debt. It's a situation that no one should have to suffer through but it's a reality that so many of us must face. What happens once a money judgment has been made?

Once a money judgment has been made, your creditor has to officially notify you and your employer of the judgment through documents sent from the court. Once your employer receives an order to alter your paycheck they are supposed to let you know before they start taking money out and giving it to your creditor. There should be a grace period for you to be able to contest the issue and or attend any hearings that involve garnishing your wages.

You should take immediate action to stop the wage garnishment before a judgment is made. (see the next chapter) Be sure to attend the court date if any so that you can explain to the judge why you should not be garnished or how you can only pay so much.

You may get lucky and the judge could grant payment arrangements, a lesser amount, or deny the wage garnishment altogether. In my opinion once you start to fight the creditor you have to be sure and follow through by being diligent; cross every T and dot every I; don't miss a beat when it comes to representing yourself.

If you still don't understand what is happening to your paycheck you may want to seek legal counsel. You may even be a victim of identity theft where the debt doesn't even belong to you. In this case you need to immediately get your documentation in order so that you can file an appeal to prove to the judge and the creditor that the debt does not belong to you.

FYI: There are two types of wage garnishments

wage garnishment, creditors can legally require your employer to hand over part of your earnings to pay off your debts.

nonwage garnishment, commonly referred to as a bank levy, creditors can tap into your bank account.

Who can garnish your wages?

If your creditor takes you to court for a debt that you rightfully owe you may be in threat of having your wages garnished if they ask the judge to do so.

One way for the creditor to most definitely win their case is if you do not show up to court and fight for your rights. If you receive a summons in the mail about possibly having your wages garnished you should never ignore it especially if you don't want to watch your hard-earned paycheck shrink.

Note: Skip to the next section about *How can I prevent wage garnishment* if you want to know immediately what to do. But right now, let's explore the few agencies that may be able to collect money from your wages through wage garnishment.

Government Agencies:

Child Support: Almost everyone knows that if you have children you are responsible for 50% of their care and if you are separated from the other parent the courts may step in and make you pay your portion of support. If support payments are ordered and you miss your payments you will be legally pursued for what you owe. If you are unemployed and ask the judge to show you mercy he just may lower your payments. But if you gain employment at any time and fail to tell the judge so that your payments can be adjusted you may face a higher wage judgment than usual but either way your wages will be collected without a doubt. This is a judgment that cannot be avoided.

Student Loans: If you attended college and took out student loans and incurred a debt you may suffer a wage judgment also. If you fail to pay monthly the student loans that you promised to pay, your wages may be affected. A way to divert payments or get rid of them altogether is to ask for a Forbearance, a deferment or an Income Based Payment Plan through the student loan agency that you owe. Some of these repayment methods may stall your payments for up to a year or longer depending on the situation. See Glossary for definitions of *Forbearance, Deferment, Income Based Payment Plan*

IRS Debt: Your wages can also be taken if you owe back income taxes to the IRS. There are ways to lower your debt with the IRS so that you can pay them in full. Locate a Tax Resolution company that is reputable and ask them for details. It may vary from state to state.

Remember, some of these government agencies can garnish your wages without a court judgment. These types of debts are called statutory garnishment because the right is created in statutory law.

Other companies that may win a wage judgment against you are:

Credit Card Companies

Personal loan Companies

Medical Bills

The number of agencies that can take advantage of what is technically referred to as a money judgement could be endless. The who, the why and to what extent all depends upon the state that you live in. Never hesitate to research the laws in your state when it comes to wage garnishment or anything that has to do with your finances period!

We never know how different companies handle their delinquencies. Some companies are nonchalant and will continue to just bill you or hand you over to a collection agency. Some companies are more serious and to the point about their collections and may want their money paid back to them in full. It depends on the situation and how much money is owed but, it's better to know ahead of time what agency you are dealing with so that you can be better prepared for what may happen to your wages.

Remember this information that you are privy too is not a tool to get out of paying bills that you owe. I wrote this book for people who are struggling due to hardship and unexpected occurrences. Or maybe this person has children and they are trying to earn a decent living but only has one income to do it with. Imagine being a single parent caring for children with no other resources except for your paycheck and then from out nowhere you are hit with a wage garnishment!

Not many people are as fortunate as others to be able to just allow a wage garnishment to happen. Credit companies extend credit for the purpose of making money and they are willing to collect their payments by any means, so don't expect sympathy cards if you can't pay!

Once again no one company will collect on their debts in the same way. You may catch a break in some areas but whichever way it goes you want to always know who you are dealing with and be prepared to go to court and plea your case if you have to.

Seven Days or Less Garnishment Killer

How to stop a creditor from garnishing you

It is so often times that people find out about a wage garnishment only after their wages have already been taken from their paycheck! How do you recover after working your hardest for 40 to 80 hours straight, get handed a check by your employer only to learn that nearly 25% of what you thought you were going to get is gone?

"Well you knew you owed a debt! Why are you so surprised?" Your employer asks you. Then with no empathy at all they turn around and tell you, "By law I am ordered by the courts to issue your creditors these funds." That's a song that would make someone want to quit their job and just give up. But since you have 2.2 kids, a car note, a mortgage and a dog to feed you can't give up because you are responsible for things and people that are way more important than that dusty old bill. A dusty bill that you probably forgot existed until the day that they started soaking up your paycheck.

How could this have happened without warning? Did you honestly forget or was it always last on your agenda? Either way the judgment was made, and it went in the favor of the creditor whoever they may be, and your loss is their gain in the form of your wages. Why didn't they send you any type of opportunity to protest, or to plea your case? How did you not know, or did you ignore the mailers and the phone calls that would have given you time to prepare for your court date?

One way to reverse a wage judgment is to file an objection. If you are responsible for more than 50% of the support of a dependent in your care you may qualify for what is called a wage garnishment exemption. Your state has a "Head of Household" exemption which lessens the amount of garnishment allowed in this situation.

As soon as you get your petition in the mail, start putting your paperwork together and prepare to prove why your wage judgment should be exempt. Certain income may be considered for exemption such as:

- Social Security
- Child Support
- Disability
- Retirement and
- Alimony

Another method of protesting your garnishment is to file an appeal. You must show just cause proving to the judge that you should not have your wages taken from your paycheck. Some reasons could be because you just cannot afford to take care of your family. Or you may not have the ability to pay for daily living expenses, or you could stand to lose your home etc.

To file an appeal, you must take thorough steps and correctly submit your documents in a timely fashion. Always check with your state to know the actual steps to take, but this is an example of how to get started.

- Reason for appeal

- Financial Statement
- File all necessary documents
- Allow time for creditor to respond
- Wait for court response

Be sure to attend any court dates if necessary

You can always talk to a lawyer and retain their services if you feel overwhelmed. A lot of people believe that they can't afford legal representation but if your wages are being garnished how can you afford not to? A lawyer will be able to help you with a convincing appeal and with filing all the legal steps that you have to take. With his/her help you may get an unfair wage judgment reversed or the amount reduced so that you can afford to financially take care of your family without wages being taken from your paycheck.

Find out from your states local clerk website your rights to object. You may have to file a written objection to the wage garnishment; the rules may vary from state to state.

Whatever you do in life you have to not let things just happen to you, you have to make things happen, it's the only way to stay successful at all you accomplish or try to do. Its okay to fail at some things but if you can help it, try to make the best of things. Don't let these companies bully you into believing that you are a bad person for falling behind on your payments. Prove to yourself that you are worthy of keeping your hard-earned money by not missing your court date.

How to File a Claim of Exemption

If you are serious about stopping your wage garnishment it would be wise to file a claim of exemption in your state. This can be done by filing a document with the court that issued the garnishment order.

- Do not forget to include in your filing your:
- Your Complete Name
- Name of the creditor that is suing you
- The case number that is on the docket that was sent to you
- Be precise in describing the type of exemption that you think might apply to you that will allow you to keep most of your wages. You will need to file your document with the clerk's office in the county where the garnishment started.

A hearing may be scheduled for you depending on your state's rules. Watch your mail for a notice of the hearing and definitely do not miss the hearing. You want every opportunity to personally explain to the judge your case. The judge will want to hear your explanation as to why you feel you deserve an exemption for specific situation.

Be sure to have every supporting document that you may need with you at the hearing. You never know if the judge will ask to see proof; even if you have more than enough paperwork…it's better to be safe than sorry.

If the judge rules in your favor he/she will order the creditor to reduce or stop garnishing your wages. But if the creditor has a convincing enough argument you will continue to get your wages garnished.

Doing paperwork especially legal paperwork can be a bit overwhelming at times. But there are resources that are available to us online that can help better guide you through the process. Although by the end of this book you will learn how to stop a garnishment within 7 days or less I wanted to give you other options. The method that I will show you can be utilized as a last resort and can help you immediately and bypass the exemption altogether. But it's good to know the prior methods I have explained just in case you do not choose to go the 7-day route.

I always want to remind the readers of this book that I am not a lawyer and I do not give legal advice. The suggestions in this book is merely steps that I have researched in my quest to stop my own wage garnishment and wanted to share it with you.

Here are some samples of forms that you may find. They may be different in each state but like I said…you would have to research your own state. Samples of wage garnishment exemption and a sample of what the document may look like from your creditor

Seven Days or Less Garnishment Killer

Claim of Exemption
Wage Garnishment Form
Sample; Forms may be different state to state…

Seven Days or Less Garnishment Killer

This is a copy of an Earnings Withholding order that you may receive in the mail explaining to you the results of your case. More than likely it will tell you how much you owe and how will be deducted to satisfy the debt.

How can I prevent Wage Garnishment?

As I stated before no one is perfect, and the world won't stop to pacify you whenever you make mistakes. The best thing that you can do is to keep on moving in the right direction and handle your issues as a mature adult by not running away from your problems.

One main way to prevent wage garnishments is pretty obvious and that is to pay your bills on time. If you fall behind it's okay…just pay what you can until you can fully catch up! We all have other obligations, but we should not neglect unpaid accounts if we can help it.

And I know that life hurdles and challenges can keep us on our toes, sometimes making it hard for us to walk a straight line within our financial map. We budget, and plan, maneuver and dodge threats of shut offs and repos on a month to month basis with little to no hope of ever catching up. But if we can somehow find a strategy to structure our finances so that we can pay each bill, every month like clockwork that just may keep us out of the wage garnishment loop.

Aside from paying bills another way to stay up to date on your debts is to make sure that you open every snail mail letter and E-mail that you receive from your creditors. Ignoring the notices and summons is an easy way to get your wages garnished.

One day you receive a court order in the mail with a judgment that says that you have to pay this and that for xyz amounts. The judgment is in the favor of your debtor and their lawyer has already made contact with your employer. You only have yourself to blame for not opening your mail.

Bottom line stay vigilant when it comes to your money you earned it and you deserve a fair trial and decision.

7- Day Breakdown

on killing a garnishment!

Okay so you made it through! You have learned all about wage garnishments, wage judgments and your right to possibly have the garnishment waved. I have enlightened you with options and steps that you can take to act on reversing any negative decision that may reflect on your hard-earned income.

We talked about agencies and companies that can legally interfere with your wages through a court order to garnish your wages, even if they are in your bank account. There are so many things that you can do to save your paycheck from being interrupted.

Even though you have been well informed about all of the above methods you are still curious to know how can I have my garnishment stopped in 7 days or less?

Since you have been such a great patient listener I won't delay your curiosity any longer. A few people may already be familiar with this garnishment killer and only few may qualify to have this procedure done.

BANKRUPTCY! That's right; filing for chapter 7 bankruptcy may eliminate your obligation to have your wages garnished. Of course, filing bankruptcy to eliminate debt is no secret, but in 10 easy simple steps you can have your garnished wages stopped in a matter of days…depending on how fast and accurate you can complete your paperwork.

I'm not going to hold you up…here are the 10 steps to a successful objection to your wage judgment utilizing chapter 7 bankruptcy.

Find the bankruptcy clerks office in your state and for your county. Ask for a bankruptcy application it should be free it may vary from state to state. You must have your driver's license so that they can issue you an application. Or you can download a bankruptcy application directly from the bankruptcy court's website.

- Complete an approved credit counseling class and a debtor education class
- Supply pay stubs for the 6 months prior to the date of filing
- Provide tax returns for 2 years if you were required to file returns
- Pass the "Means Test," which is a detailed budget analysis of your income and expenses

Read the entire packet thoroughly before putting pen to paper. There should be instructions that come along with it to explain how to fill out each schedule. Follow all the instructions to the letter this is very important. Missing information can leave you to start all over or stall your case.

Get your credit report from all three credit agencies. Using sites like credit Karma will not have a complete listing of your entire credit report so be sure to get the reports directly from each agency's website. Using annualcreditreport.com will be a better choice. Look over your report for inaccuracies and for anything that is accurate you will want to include into your bankruptcy paperwork.

Complete the entire bankruptcy application filling out the schedules one by one carefully; try not to make any or many mistakes this could cause a delay. Do not forget to exempt your property in your schedule C. You will need information about income and expenses, so dig up all of your bills and check stubs to include in your filing.

Transfer information from your credit reports to your bankruptcy application. Be sure to include all debtors, any collection agencies connected to your debts, hospital bills, traffic tickets or whatever you can possibly include that you think you may owe.

Utilize law-based web sites that have a general knowledge of bankruptcies and the schedules that you are completing. You will be surprised to find that most of these sights will have a wealth of information that is generated based on your state. Even if you get a little stuck; ask the right question in the web site's search and you may get lucky and find the right answer.

Bankruptcy Courses are required to complete the bankruptcy. These common-sense courses are not included in your bankruptcy documents. They are mostly online and will cost anywhere between $10-$25 (I wouldn't pay more than that) These trusted sites can be found on the bankruptcy website in your district. Once you complete the course do not…I stress do not forget to print the certificate of completion that they are going to E-mail to you.

☆ **Submit Your application**. If you follow the instructions to the letter and fill out your schedules quickly and accurately you are well on your way to **getting your wage garnishment stopped.**

Ex: If you finish and submit your paperwork within in seven days or less. (it can be done) The clerks will process your information within 30 minutes…at which point a case number is then generated for your case. An *Automatic Stay* goes into effect immediately…this means that by law all your creditors must not bill you for collections until after a decision at your meeting of creditors. This includes the wage garnishment.

Attend Meeting of Creditors. You will probably get a date for court the same day that you submit your paperwork. To remind you they will send you a copy of your petition with the location and time of your court hearing. A trustee will hear your case and if your creditors don't show up…you may pretty much win your case. For the most part they almost never show, but if they do…I would make sure that I have all my paperwork with me and be ready to plea to the judge my situation. Don't be afraid to represent yourself…you know you better than anyone else. Just be as honest and humble as you can be.

They should be able to tell you the same day as your hearing as long as you win and, as long as you have paid all of the fees associated with the case and you have submitted all of your necessary paperwork your bankruptcy should probably be discharged 30 days from the date that you had your meeting of creditors. Good luck I hope this helps everyone who really needs it!

Bonus!

10 things Lawyers don't want you know about filing your own bankruptcy!

1. You can save thousands of dollars filing your own bankruptcy (some states don't apply check with your local bankruptcy district)

2. You can represent yourself in a court of law including bankruptcies (wouldn't recommend for Chapter 13 but it can be done)

3. Court cost in some states can be divided into payments. As long as you make timely payments you can still have your bankruptcy discharged. (you may even be able to ask for an extension) If you don't pay all of the payments your case may get dismissed.

4. All of the information that a lawyer knows about bankruptcy is free and online. You just

have to know where to look and the right questions to ask Google.

5. You can amend a bankruptcy. Say for instance that the bankruptcy trustee happens to utilize your tax return because you fail to include it properly in your exemptions. You can amend your bankruptcy (fix the error) which may lead to the trustee returning your tax money back to you.

6. You may qualify for a fee waiver. You must pay filing fee to file your bankruptcy but, in some cases, depending on your income situation the courts may grant you a waiver and you don't have to pay. If you do your

own bankruptcy successfully and are allowed a waiver, you would have completed your bankruptcy for free.

7. You can ask for a reaffirmation of your debt. Say for instance that you have a car that you are making payments on you may be able to negotiate a new contract so that your car won't be pulled into the bankruptcy.

8. You can exempt your property including but not limited to: household goods, clothing, electronics, jewelry, 401k, other pensions, and more. You can even exempt tax returns also.

9. There may be a what is called a Pro Se' Clerk that can assist you at the physical bankruptcy office. The clerk can critique and grade your bankruptcy documents and can tell you without advising your legally (which they cannot do) as to if your schedules are completed correctly before submitting it the clerk

10. Some lawyers are amazingly helpful and are willing to answer a few of your questions. But they can only answer so much knowing that you have not retained their services. They don't want to be legally liable for the way that you complete your schedules,

but I believe you have nothing to worry about.

Good luck once again and I wish you a *Happy Bankruptcy Day! #keepyourmoney #stopthegarnishment!*

Conclusion

That was such an exciting journey to take with you guys. It was such a pleasure to make someone's day by providing them with the power to keep their earnings from getting garnished.

Prayerfully this information will lead people to research and re-read as much as they can about this subject so that whatever they are going through the issues can be resolved.

My disclaimer included in this publication is that I am not a Lawyer and I do not give legal advice. This book is a reflection of how I personally handled a wage garnishment through bankruptcy!

To recap, a wage garnishment is a successful judgment against any individual that owes a debt to a company or government agency. The courts can order for the money to be taken out of your paycheck or directly from your bank account.

If you are experiencing a hardship due to wage garnishment or are on a fixed income you may be able to object to the garnishment by filing an objection or exemption. Details for filing such pleadings may be researched online. Lawyer websites have so many different details about bankruptcies and garnishments you will have to do your research once again.

If you feel overwhelmed by the paperwork and the procedures of bankruptcy & wage garnishment, or you are afraid that you are going to mess up, please seek legal counsel. Lawyers are not a bad thing…but if you are patient enough to get through the steps of dissolving yourself of your wage garnishment you can save so much money.

Being mindful of your finances and creating and sticking to structured realistic budgets may keep you from wage garnishment in the first place. No one is perfect but paying any amount to your creditors will keep you from being late. So, try your best to make it work the way that you know how.

I want everyone to be blessed and have a wonderful life! If this book was helpful and you want to learn more don't hesitate to visit us online at www.thewomensbookshelf.com! Thanks for your interest in our publications, be reading with you soon!

Glossary

Appeal- apply to a higher court for a reversal of the decision of a lower court

Automatic Stay- is the injunction a bankruptcy filing places on all creditors and debt collection agencies. What this means is they are prohibited from attempting to contact you.

Budget- an estimate of income and expenditure for a set period

Chapter 7 Bankruptcy- a liquidation bankruptcy that wipes out most of your general unsecured debts such as credit cards and medical bills without the need to pay back balances through a repayment plan

Chapter 13 Bankruptcy- a reorganization bankruptcy designed for debtors with regular income who have enough left over each month to pay back at least a portion of their debts through a repayment plan.

Child Support- court-ordered payments, typically made by a noncustodial divorced parent, to support one's minor child or children.

Creditors- A creditor is an entity, a company or a person of a legal nature that has provided goods, services, or a monetary loan to a debtor

Debt- something, typically money, that is owed or due

Deductions- the action of deducting or subtracting something

Deferment- the action or fact of putting something off to a later time; postponement

Delinquencies- Failure to make a payment on a debt or obligation by the specified due date.

Exemption- the process of freeing or state of being free from an obligation or liability imposed on others

Filing- the entering of a legal document into the public record

Forbearance- An agreement to temporarily postpone or suspend a borrower's payments

Hardship- a situation in which a person cannot keep up with debt payments and bills.

Hearings- A judge in a civil court hearing decides several kinds of legal issues.

Income Based Payment Plan- a repayment plan that caps your required monthly payments on the major types of federal student loans at an amount intended to be affordable based on income and family size

Levies- A levy allows a creditor to withdraw money from a financial account—most commonly, a checking or savings account

Legal counsel- A lawyer or attorney is a person who practices law, as an advocate, attorney, attorney at law

Liens- A lien is a notice attached to your property telling the world that a creditor claims you owe it some money.

Means Test- determine whether an individual debtor's chapter 7 filing can be presumed to be an abuse of the Bankruptcy Code requiring dismissal or conversion of the case.

Non-wage garnishment-commonly referred to as a bank levy, creditors can tap into your bank account.

Objection- meaning they are objecting something said by the other lawyer, company or person suing

Petition-petition is a formal written request to have a legal matter heard and decided by the court.

Pro Se'- Latin phrase meaning on one's own behalf or for himself. This typically refers to an individual who represents one's self in court.

Re-affirmation- In Chapter 7 bankruptcy, one way to keep the property is to reaffirm the debt. You and the lender will enter into a reaffirmation agreement and file it with the court.

Tax Resolution- Tax debt relief or consolidation

Wages- a fixed regular payment, typically paid on a daily or weekly basis, made by an employer to an employee, especially to a manual or unskilled worker

Wage Garnishment/Judgment- creditors can legally require your employer to hand over part of your earnings to pay off your debts.

Thank you for your interest in this publication. There will be many more to come touching base on topics that can assist people like you and me in financially gaining our footing, one step at a time.

Thanks to online resources such as:

Google

Youtube

Nolo.com

& Wikipedia

All rights reserved © 2018
The Women's Bookshelf Ent.

www.ingramcontent.com/pod-product-compliance
Lightning Source LLC
Chambersburg PA
CBHW070956240526
45469CB00016B/1445